# Write On Target

## Practical Advice
## From Real Teachers

written by Cindy Merrilees and Pamela Haack

Illustrated by R. Michael Palan

To Jay, Ben, Michael and Melissa; and Daddy, Mama, Karen, Michael, Jimmy, Denise, Timmy and Donald.

My immediate family . . . my foundation.

C.M.

To Mom and Dad for their tremendous support, Terri for being so proud of her little sister, and Tony for his constant encouragement.

P.H.

# TABLE OF CONTENTS

# Introduction

—Do you feel pressured by teaching writing?

—Do you feel you don't have time to write with your class every day?

—Are you at a loss for ideas when it comes to writing?

—Are your students less than enthusiastic about writing?

—Are you less than enthusiastic about writing?

—Do you CRINGE when you hear the words "Creative Writing"?

If you answered yes to any of the above questions, then this is your lucky day! You are now reading the very book that may make your life easier . . . and change your attitude about writing!

As classroom teachers, we too have experienced the feelings of frustration and doubt that are associated with teaching writing.

However, as elementary teachers become more aware of the effectiveness of whole language instruction, we realize the importance of daily writing in the classroom. We have also seen firsthand the creativity and excitement that our students show as they write, write, write!

Through our experiences as classroom teachers, we have come up with what we think are some practical ways to begin to implement daily writing activities. This book is intended to be a starting point for teachers and/or students who are new to the writing process. We know from our experience how intimidating writing can be in the beginning stages.

As you use the ideas presented in this book, you and your students will begin to feel comfortable and successful. This will give you the confidence to explore the writing process further, and move into more self-directed, independent writing activities.

Teachers will stick with those ideas that they are most comfortable with, and that overburden them the least. So, give our ideas a try, and see how easy writing can be. But remember, our ideas are just to get you started. We hope you will explore areas of writing that encourage your students to go further and further with their thoughts, ideas, and creativity. We know you will have fun, and we hope you will stick with it!

# Individual Books

# Individual Books

An easy and organized way to incorporate daily writing into your classroom is to write a book every week. Don't panic! It's really not as hard as it sounds. Our students write **individual books** and **whole-group books.** The individual books are done on a weekly basis, and the whole-group books are done occasionally.

This structured "book-writing time" is not the only writing that is done in our classrooms. You will find many other opportunities to incorporate writing into your day. However, we feel it is also beneficial to have a daily writing routine.

**Individual books** are those books your children will write individually each week. Twenty minutes is set aside each day, in our classrooms, as "book-writing time." All your students can complete a book of their own, each week, using the following steps:

## Day One — Brainstorming

Familiarize your students with the "format of the week." Begin brainstorming out loud and write the ideas on the chalkboard.

## Day Two — Rough Draft

Continue brainstorming, and have students begin writing their ideas down on a rough draft copy while you circulate and help students correct spelling, punctuation, sentence structure, grammar, etc. Keep in mind that inventive spelling is important in primary grades, and should be encouraged. Use your own judgment as to the extent of editing you do. You don't want to discourage children from writing!

## Day Three — Begin Final Copies

Students begin transferring their ideas to a final copy. The final copies we use are made by stapling 8 1/2" x 11" plain white paper inside a piece of 9" x 12" folded construction paper, forming a small booklet. (See instructions on pages 10-12.) Students begin by designing their cover and title pages, and by making a dedication and copyright page. Then they transfer the words from their rough drafts into their booklets while you continue to circulate and assist.

## Day Four — Complete Final Copies

Students continue transferring ideas from the rough draft copies to their booklets.

## Day Five — Sharing

Allow students to read their completed books to your class and other classes throughout the school. Then the students can take the books home and share them with their families. They love this part!

# Whole-Group Books

# Whole-Group Books

To add variety to your daily writing schedule, take a week off from writing individual books and write a whole-group book. In this activity, the children will contribute one page to a class book instead of writing individual books. This writing will be done during the same twenty-minute period that we call "book-writing time." However, it is not necessary to use the five-day schedule we use when writing individual books. This gives you a chance to be creative and try something different.

Also, making these books oversized would be an inexpensive way to add "big books" to your classroom library.

As with individual books, you will spend the first day familiarizing your students with the format. This is when you'll use brainstorming to get everyone involved and get the ideas rolling.

The rest of the week you will circulate while your students work on their rough drafts and then their final pages.

You may choose to write the words onto the final copy for your students, or have them copy their own words. This will depend on the grade level you teach. Another option is to let students copy their own words in pencil and trace over them yourself with marker.

The illustrations will always be done by the students themselves, and can be done using a variety of media including:

  a. crayon with watercolor wash
  b. construction paper cutouts
  c. tempera paint
  d. watercolors
  e. markers
  f. colored chalk
  g. oil pastels

Add to the uniqueness of each book by using different binding techniques, such as
  a. using brass fasteners
  b. tying the pages together with yarn
  c. sewing the pages in by hand or by machine
  (see instructions that follow)
  d. binding the pages with a binding machine. (If your school doesn't have one, put in your request NOW! It's a must for every school.)

You will find that these class-made books will not only be the most popular books in your reading center, but every child will be able to read them. After all, they wrote them! Your students will also be thrilled if you let them make a copy of their own to take home. (See page 16.)

## Instructions For Sewn Books

### Hand sewn:

These directions will make a 10" x 14" book with 24 pages.

### Materials Needed:

1 piece of cardboard (14" x 20")
7 pieces of construction paper (12" x 18")
1 strip of construction paper (4" x 18")
wallpaper scraps
glue
embroidery needle
string

### Directions:

1. Fold cardboard in half, open, and lay on back side of wallpaper scraps.

2. Fold and glue wallpaper scraps around outside of front and back covers, leaving a 3" gap on the fold.

3. Glue 4" strip of construction paper along gap on outside cover, folding ends into the middle of the cover.

4. Glue one piece of 12" x 18" construction paper on inside cover to hide rough edges.

5. Fold remaining six pieces of construction paper together, and sew into cover using embroidery needle and string.

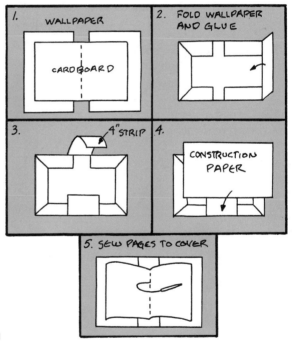

## Machine Sewn:

These instructions will make a 10" x 14" book with 24 pages.

## Materials Needed:

2 pieces of cardboard (10" x 14")
7 pieces of construction paper (12" x 18")
1 piece of contact paper (18" x 24")
glue
sewing machine
transparent tape

## Directions:

1. Lay contact paper on table and remove backing (sticky side up).

2. Place two pieces of cardboard on contact paper, leaving even margins and a 1/2" gap for the center fold.

3. Fold edges of contact paper over top and bottom of cardboard.

4. Clip edges at an angle.

5. Fold in sides of contact paper and tape to secure.

6. Fold the seven pieces of construction paper in half to make a center crease.

7. Unfold pages and sew together along center crease line on sewing machine (use a long stitch).

8. Spread glue on entire inside of cover and glue sewn pages into cover.

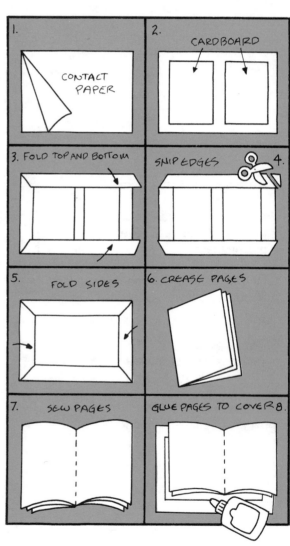

# Helpful Hints:
# Daily Writing Made Easy

# Helpful Hints:
# Daily Writing Made Easy

When we first attempted to write with our students every day, we encountered some problems. We weren't having much fun . . . and neither were they. So, we were forced to find solutions to those problems, to help regain our sanity!

Listed below are some common problems that you might also encounter as you begin daily writing with your class. Along with these problems, we have listed possible solutions. We hope that this will spare you some frustration.

**Problem:** "You expect me to make a booklet for every student in my class to write in, for every week of the year? Let's see . . . 27 kids, times 36 weeks . . . THAT'S NEARLY 1000 BOOKS!"

**Solution:** The booklets we use are simply a few pieces of paper (8 1/2" x 11"), folded inside a piece of construction paper (9" x 12"), stapled down the folded side.

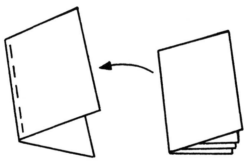

(Surely you have several "little helpers" who can't seem to do enough for you. Let them fold and staple your booklets for you ahead of time. Another alternative is to allow your students to construct their own booklets, with the amount of pages needed for their book.)

**Problem**: "Teacher, I can't think of anything to write!"

**Solution**: Each time you begin a book, it is important to familiarize students with the format that will be used. The next step is to begin brainstorming. This is when the students share ideas aloud. As you know, hearing another person's ideas helps to spark your own imagination. Some children need that extra push to get started, and after brainstorming, will feel more at ease.

**Problem**: "My students can't seem to get their writing materials organized!"

**Solution**: Students should have a two-pocket folder to use as their "writing folder." Rough drafts can be kept on one side of the folder, final copies on the other. Frequently used words, such as *dedication, copyright, written* and *illustrated,* can be written directly on the folder also.

**Problem**: "Teacher, how do you spell _____, and how do you spell _____, and how do you spell _____?"

**Solution:** To avoid spending all your time answering this question, simply encourage your students to spell the words as best they can, and to circle any words they think are misspelled. Frequently misspelled words can also be written in the "writing folder."

**Problem:** "Jeremy, it has been 30 minutes and you have nothing on your paper!"

**Solution:** We all have a student, or two, who wishes to do as little as possible, as often as possible. We offer no miracle solutions. However, we do use motivational techniques to turn these children on, such as
   a. an offer to read their book to another class
   b. praise for working to their potential, rather than the potential of other students
   c. reminders that their books go home to people who will cherish them
   d. positive reinforcement when they apply themselves. "Catch them doing well" and tell the whole world about it.

**Problem:** "Teacher, I'm finished. What do I do now?"

**Solution:** For those students who always finish first (you know . . . the child who finishes the assignment before you finish giving the directions), have some additional activities on hand. As a reward for doing good work in a timely manner, let them choose from the following activities:
   a. making a duplicate book for the reading center
   b. reading their book to another class
   c. writing a story or poem "on their own"
   d. making a duplicate book for their teacher
   e. writing in their journal
   f. writing on a topic of their choice

**Problem:** "I know I'll have some students who will only write a few pages, and some who would write a novel, if I let them. How will I accommodate both?"

**Solution:** The simplicity of a construction paper and plain white paper booklet allows you to add or subtract pages as needed. But remember, it's perfectly all right for some children to write less than others because they are working to their individual potentials.

**Problem:** "How can my 28 students share one copy of a whole-group book?"

**Solution:** When making a whole-group book, (which means there will be only one copy of the book), you will find that your students will fight over that one copy. Some will also want to take the book home to share with their families. To prevent "World War III," and possibly a torn-up book, simply make copies on a copy machine for each child. Let them make their own covers, cut out the pages, and color the illustrations if they wish. (Some books may need to be copied on a reduction copier to be made into a small copy of the original book.)

If you choose not to make individual copies of a whole-group book, you may wish to send the one copy home on a check-out basis. It's nice to add a page at the back for parents' comments.

**Problem:** "How do I assess my students' writing?"

**Solution:** We prefer not to use formal grading on our students' books. However, informally, you will be assessing your students' use of grammar, punctuation, spelling, sentence structure, and of course, the content of their books every time they write. Depending on your school/district requirement, you may use assessment tools such as check lists, portfolios, profile sheets, teacher narratives, etc.

# Idea-A-Week: Book Ideas For The Entire School Year

September

October

November

December

January

February

March

April

May

# Idea-A-Week:Book Ideas
# For The Entire School Year

One of the most difficult aspects of daily writing is coming up with new and exciting ideas. Since your students will be writing books each week, you will need to be prepared. We decided we needed to get organized after several weeks of coming into our classrooms on Monday morning and saying, "Oh my gosh! I don't have an idea for a book this week!" The result was a list of book ideas, neatly compiled by week, for each of the nine school months.

This section contains that list, along with actual examples written by our students. We hope this proves to be a useful reference and that it might spare you that "Monday Morning Panic" that we experienced.

You might also wish to encourage your students to generate ideas for books. As we all know, many times their ideas are much better than those we come up with.

# September

## My ABC Book
### (Whole-Group Book)

### Start the year with an easy book.

**Format:** Each student chooses one letter of the alphabet and a word or sentence and illustration to go along with that letter.

**Examples:**

- The finished product is a great reference when teaching beginning sounds.

- Individual copies of this book could be used as student dictionaries, with room for additional words.

- This would be a great way to teach alliteration to students in upper grades.

# The Never Book
## (Individual Book)

### Words that rhyme make this book fun.

**Format:** Students choose two rhyming words that describe something they should never do.

**Examples:**

**Suggested endings:**
But always . . .
But never, never, never . . .

---

• More formats using rhyming words:

Could you _____ a _____?
(Example: Could you scare a bear?)

A _____ with a _____
(Example: A cat with a hat)

• What a great opportunity to share Dr. Seuss books with your class!

---

# Yum!
## (Individual Book)

**Use beginning consonant sounds in a yummy (maybe yucky) way.**

**Format:** Students choose two foods that begin with the same letter.

**Examples:**

**Suggested endings:**
But my very favorite food is . . .
But the food I like the best is . . .

- This is a fun book to write when you teach the four food groups. (Example: List one food from each food group on the same page.)

- Students could bring in their favorite foods.

- When teaching the five senses, have a "taste test" day, using foods from these books.

# The Storm Book
## (Whole-Group Book)

### Watch out! Stormy weather ahead!

**Format:** Discuss and read about storms, focusing on the types of storms that are common in your region. Each child chooses a storm-related topic and writes a paragraph about that topic.

**Examples:**

**Tornadoes**

Tornadoes are bad storms. First the sky turns black, then the wind starts twirling. It moves across land and drops on certain places.

**Hurricanes**

Hurricanes are dangerous because of strong winds. They form over the ocean. They make lots of rain.

The Storm Book

### Suggested Endings:
The last page should be one that summarizes the book, such as
   a page on storms in general
   a conclusion stating the dangers of storms.

---

• Storm books could be a great culmination to a weather unit.

• To incorporate current events, have students bring in newspaper articles about the weather.

•Follow up this book by charting local weather. Encourage students to watch the news.

# October

## Sometimes I Forget
### (Individual Book)

**Sometimes we remember,
And sometimes we forget.**

**Format:** Students think of things they remember and things they forget. (If they have a hard time coming up with ideas, tell them to think of things they get in trouble for at home!)

**Examples:**

I remember to brush my teeth but I forget to turn off the water.

I remember to do my homework but I forget to turn it in.

**Suggested Endings:**

But I always remember to . . .
And I always forget to . . .
But I never forget to . . .

---

- Before writing, read Mercer Mayer's *I Just Forgot*.

- Have students role-play various situations.

- Bring in books about improving your memory, and practice these techniques with your students.

# Fortunately/Unfortunately

## (Individual Book)

### Some days just go that way.

**Format:** Students fill in the format:

"Unfortunately _____. Fortunately _____."

**Examples:**

Fortunately I got a new bike!
Unfortunately it has a flat tire.

Fortunately I found a dollar!
Unfortunately I lost it again.

**Suggested Endings:**

But I was very fortunate when . . .

But it's better than fortune . . .

And most fortunately . . .

- Share Remy Charlip's book, *Fortunately, Unfortunately*.

- Discuss optimism and pessimism with your students.

- *The Little Engine That Could* is a perfect book to illustrate making fortune from misfortune.

# Facts About Bats
## (Individual Book)

**Bats are interesting mammals to study this time of year.**

**Format:** Discuss and read about bats. Students then write one "bat fact" on each page of their book.

**Examples:**

**Suggested Endings:**
The most interesting thing I learned about bats . . .
I think bats are . . .

---

• Books with "bat facts" are a great wrap-up of your study of mammals.

• Any art activities related to bats would be appropriate at this time, such as bat mobiles, wall mural of a cave with bats, etc.

• Informational charts and graphs listing types of bats, foods they eat, characteristics, etc.

# The Pumpkin Book
## (Whole-Group Book)

### Halloween suggests a change of pace.

**Format:** Each child contributes one page to this whole-group project by writing a four-line verse about pumpkins. (Note: Because the book is written in numerical order, the first line is given. The words on lines two and four must rhyme.)

**Examples:**

**Suggested Ending:**
All the pumpkins got together
And then they started to scream,
"We hope you all have fun tonight
And a Happy Halloween!"

---

• An unrhyming alternative to this book would be one in which the students simply write their thoughts about the holiday.

• Entertain other classes in the school during the week of Halloween by having children read their pages out loud.

• Enhance illustrations in the book with movable parts or pop-ups.

# November

## All About Me
### (Individual Book)

**Help your students learn how unique and special they are.**

**Format:** Students write information about themselves, including

a. hair and eye color
b. birthday
c. family members
d. address and phone number

e. pets
f. favorite foods
g. any other information

**Examples:**

This is my house.

My favorite food is pizza.

**Suggested Endings:**
This is me, and I'm special!
And this is me with my favorite people — my family!

---

- All About Me is a great companion to a class or school safety program in which children are encouraged to memorize their addresses, phone numbers, etc.

- This would be a perfect book to send to a pen pal in another state.

- Have a scavenger hunt where students find other students who have similar information.
(Example: Find three people with the same color hair; find someone with same favorite food.)

---

# The First Thanksgiving
## (Individual Book)

### Combine a history lesson and a fun writing activity.

**Format:** Discuss the events surrounding the first Thanksgiving. Each page will list one of these events.

**Examples:**

**Suggested Endings:**

The Pilgrims had a lot to be thankful for . . .

The first Thanksgiving was special because . . .

- Role-play the Thanksgiving story as a prewriting activity.

- There are numerous filmstrips, books, and videos available to initiate discussion on the first day of writing.

- Have students read their books aloud during a class Thanksgiving feast.

# Thankful Poems

## (Whole-Group Book)

### What are you the most thankful for?

**Format:** Students each write a poem for this class book. The first line states their name. The second line states a characteristic. The third line is given. The fourth line rhymes with line two.

**Examples:**

> Said Anna Cohen
> With the green-blue eyes
> I am thankful for
> the pumpkin pies

> Said Randy Wells
> With brown hair
> I am thankful for
> All the people that care

Thankful Poems

---

• An unrhymed alternative would be one in which your students simply write about things they are thankful for.

• An idea for this book's cover is to have each child make one of the feathers on a turkey.

• Children could make individual books using their handprint for the turkey cover.

# I Hate It When That Happens

## (Individual Book)

### Have you ever had "one of those days"?

**Format:** Students think of those things that could ruin their day. Each page ends with the phrase: "I hate it when that happens!"

**Examples:**

**Suggested Endings:**
But I love it when . . .
. . . I love it when that happens!

---

- This book idea can be used with any other familiar phrase. (Examples: Cowabunga! Totally awesome! Are we there yet?)

- Read *Alexander and the Terrible, Horrible, No Good, Very Bad Day* by Judith Viorst.

- Follow up on this book with a writing activity about "The Best Day Ever."

# December

## Good For Me
### (Individual Book)

**Wow! Look what I did!**

**Format:** Students think of things that they are proud of.

**Examples:**

**Suggested Endings:**
. . . Good for you!
. . . Boy, am I good!

---

• Have students boast about their accomplishments by bringing in trophies, awards, certificates, etc.

• A great way to get parents involved would be to send home a "positive behavior check list" for them to complete and return for their child.

• This would be a great time to visit the biography section in your school library to study people who are known for their great accomplishments.

---

# Memories Of Christmas
## (Whole-Group Book)

### Do you remember your favorite Christmas?

**Format:** Each child writes one page that describes a Christmas he/she will always remember. The pages are put together to form a book. The children make their own copies of the book to take home for the holidays.

**Examples:**

I remember baking Christmas Cookies with Mom and Grandma.

I got a new bike from Santa. It was blue and white.

Memories of Christmas

---

• A great read-aloud that helps us to focus on the true meaning of Christmas is *The Best Christmas Pageant Ever* by Barbara Robinson.

• A festive cover for this book can be made by using tissue paper and ribbon. (Twist small squares of green tissue paper around the end of a pencil, and glue onto paper to form a wreath.)

# If I Was . . .
## (Individual Book)

### Create a holiday book that's fun and festive!

**Format:** Students imagine themselves as holiday characters or objects. They simply fill in the blank: If I was a _____, I would _____.

**Examples:**

**Suggested Endings:**

But since I'm me . . .

But most of all, if I was . . .

---

• For a more in-depth book, have your students write a whole book about one object or character they choose.

• Role-play the parts of inanimate objects.
(Example: Have students draw the name of an object from a hat, and pretend to be that object.)

• Have students share their books during your Christmas program.

---

# January

## New Year's Resolutions
### (Whole-Group Book)

### Start the new year off right!

**Format:** Discuss the tradition of New Year's resolutions. The students then write their own resolutions and the pages are bound together as a class book.

**Examples:**

- As a literature tie-in, have students think of what resolutions might be made by literary characters they know.

- Use charting or graphing to document students' success with keeping their resolutions.

- Run off copies of each page for every child, and let him or her make covers for a book to take home.

# Dinosaurs
## (Individual Book)

**Children love dinosaurs. They will also love to write about them.**

**Format:** Before writing this book, expose your students to dinosaurs, dinosaurs, and more dinosaurs! Then simply let them write about dinosaurs.

**Examples:**

Some dinosaurs are meat eaters and some are plant eaters.

There are no more dinosaurs. They are extinct.

**Suggested Endings:**
I think dinosaurs died because . . .
My favorite dinosaur is . . .

- Each child may wish to do research on dinosaurs or a related topic and then write about it in detail.

- Be sure to use the latest research on this topic through the use of current magazines, newspapers, or journals.

- A great follow-up art activity would be to make dinosaurs from clay or dough.

# Expressions
## (Individual Book)

### Eek! But Mom! Oops! Oh no! Wow!

**Format:** Ask each student to think of a short expression that could be used throughout a book, such as the ones listed above. Students then think of situations that would go along with the expression.

**Examples:** (Note: The title of each book comes from the expression chosen.)

**Suggested Endings:**
Wow! Wow! Wow!
But, best of all . . . Wow!

• As a literature tie-in use books such as Mercer Mayer's *Me Too, Baby Sister Says No,* and Wright Group's big book, *Just This Once.*

• Encourage choral reading by the class when the expression is read.

# When It's Cold Outside
### (Individual Book)

## What do you like to do when it's cold outside?

**Format:** After talking about cold day activities, students choose their favorites to write about in their books.

**Examples:**

**Suggested Endings:**
But my favorite thing to do when it's cold . . .
But if it was warm outside . . .

- As a prewriting activity, play charades by role-playing cold weather activities.

- Be sure to read these books on a cold day while sipping hot chocolate.

- The perfect read-aloud to use as a companion to this activity is Harry Mazer's *Snow Bound*.

# February

## Valentine Poems
### (Whole-Group Book)

**Roses are red, violets are blue,
Writing this book will be fun for you!**

**Format:** Use the familiar rhyme: Roses are red, violets are blue. Ask your students to think of two things and their colors. Then explain to them that the last words on lines two and four must rhyme.

**Examples:**

- Students could also write an individual unrhymed book, in which they write a valentine for someone else (outside the class, some family member, etc.), saying what they like about that person.

- Before writing, be sure to read *Don't Be My Valentine* by Joan M. Lexau or *How Spider Saved Valentine's Day* by Robert Kraus.

# Just Say No!
### (Individual Book)

## Teach your students to say no to drugs.

**Format:** Write this book after discussing the dangers of drugs. Students will think of dangerous situations they could find themselves in.

**Examples:**

**Suggested Endings:**
. . . Just Say Yes!
Whenever it comes to drugs, just say no!

---

- This is a super book to write in association with red-ribbon week.

- Bring in a person from your local sheriff's department or another authority to discuss drug awareness with your students.

- An alternative topic for teachers who don't find drug issues appropriate for their class at this time would be a class safety book.

---

# My Emotions Book
## (Individual Book)

**Students need an opportunity to write about their feelings.**

**Format:** Students think of situations that make them feel certain ways.

**Examples:**

**Suggested Endings:**
But I'm most happy when . . .
No matter how I feel . . .

- This book should be written after a lengthy discussion on emotions.

- There are many books available that deal with this subject. Some of our favorites are *I'll Always Love You* by Hans Wilhelm, *A Bargain for Frances* by Russell Hoban, and many Berenstain Bears and Bill Peet books.

# People At Work
### (Individual Book)

**Write about those hardworking folks out there.**

**Format:** Begin by discussing careers with your students. Have them share information about different jobs, and use that information for their own books.

**Examples:**

**Suggested Endings:**
But the hardest job is . . .
The thing I like best about this job is . . .

• An exciting follow-up activity would be to host a career day at your school. Students could dress up for different occupations, and invited guests could share information about their careers.

• Before students write, have them interview parents, neighbors, other relatives, etc.

# March

## My Special Person
### (Individual Book)

**We all have that special someone.**

**Format:** Have students think of a person (living or not living) who means a lot to them. Then have them write about these special people who have touched their lives.

**Examples:**

When I was little, I stayed with my Aunt Sylvia.

We played a lot and ate ice cream.

**Suggested Endings:**

_____ means a lot to me.

_____ is my special person.

---

- Invite as many special people as possible to visit your classroom, or have students bring in their pictures.

- Great literature tie-ins would be *Through Grandpa's Eyes* by Patricia MacLachlan, and *The Wednesday Surprise* by Eve Bunting.

# Space
## (Whole-Group Book)

### Space . . . the final frontier.

**Format:** Each child chooses a space-related topic such as planets, sun, stars, constellations, moons, space travel, galaxies, or the universe. The page will consist of a paragraph and illustration of the topic.

**Examples:**

**MARS**

Mars is the fourth planet from the sun. It is a very rocky planet with mountains. Viking went to Mars and took pictures. Mars is reddish.

**GALAXIES**

Galaxies are a big group of stars. Billions of stars make a galaxy. Our galaxy is the Milky Way. It is a spiral galaxy.

• You may wish to incorporate report-writing skills such as research, outlining, summarizing, etc.

• Great follow-up art activities include papier-mâché planets to hang in your room, solar system mobiles made with Styrofoam balls, clay or dough models of various spacecraft.

# The Four Seasons
## (Individual Book)

**Winter, spring, summer, and fall,
This book has it all!**

**Format:** Spring is a perfect time to study the four seasons. In this book, children write about weather, surroundings, clothing, and activities related to each season.

**Examples:**

**Suggested Endings:**
But my favorite season is . . .
All the seasons . . .

---

- Students may wish to write about more focused aspects of one season, or about one topic throughout different seasons.
(Example: Favorite things to do in different seasons)

- Decorate each of your four classroom walls as one of the four seasons.

---

# Idioms
## (Individual Book)

**Our crazy use of language can be a fun study.**

**Format:** Students write idiomatic expressions and illustrate them literally.

**Examples:**

**Suggested Endings:**
My favorite idiom is . . .
An idiom I made up is . . .

- The Amelia Bedelia books by Peggy Parish are perfect for teaching idiomatic expressions.

- Play a game of charades using suggested idioms.

- This would be a great time to discuss the inconsistencies of the English language.

# April

## The Bunny Book
### (Whole-Group Book)

**Bunnies are everywhere this time of the year.
Why not write about them?**

**Format:** Each child contributes one page to this whole-group project by writing a page about bunnies. (Note: Because the book is written in numerical order, the first words are given.)

**Examples:**

- Your students would be thrilled to hold a real live bunny! Maybe a parent would volunteer to bring one in.

- Be sure to write this book before Easter, so that each of your students can take home a copy for the holiday.

- Stretched cotton balls glued to the cover make a nice soft bunny.

# The Great State Of _____

## (Individual Book)

### Students write about the state they live in.

**Format:** Teach your students about your state. Then have them write interesting "state facts" in their book.

**Examples:**

**Suggested Endings:**

The most interesting fact about Florida . . .

I like living in Florida because . . .

• This book will be one of "state facts." The individualization will lie in the artwork on the cover and pages. (It's all right to simply teach facts. Too many times we overlook them!)

• Make a class relief map of your state using flour and water.

# The Ugly _____

## (Individual Book)

### The children give renditions of an old folktale.

**Format:** Read or tell the class the story of "The Ugly Duckling." Now let your students write their own story using a different character.

**Examples:**

The mother dinosaur looked at her eggs, but one looked different.

When the eggs hatched, one baby was very ugly.

**Suggested Endings:**

And when the baby dinosaur found others like him . . .

. . . and they lived happily ever after.

- Folktale format is less structured and allows for more creativity at this time of the school year.

- Since this story has an underlying moral, a great companion would be *Aesop's Fables.*

- This book is a great introduction to folktales and fairy tales.

# When Parents Were Young
## (Individual Book)

### Students get a chance to interview Dad or Mom.

**Format:** Students will interview their parents or guardians. They will ask what things were like when that person was young. (Examples: How different were clothing, music, hair styles, recreation, world events, etc.?)

**Examples:**

**Suggested Endings:**

The thing Mom misses most about those days . . .

The thing that surprised me most about Dad . . .

---

- Be sure to teach interviewing techniques before writing this book.

- Have students recreate their parents' time period by bringing in music, old clothes, pictures of hair styles, etc. (Example: You could have a '50s sock hop and invite parents to come!)

# May

## Mother's Day
### (Individual Book)

### The perfect Mother's Day gift!

**Format:** Students write about their terrific moms. Each student thinks about when Mom is the prettiest, the happiest, the nicest, etc. (Remember, stepmoms, grandmothers, aunts, guardians, and Mr. Moms count, too!)

**Examples:**

Mom is the proudest when I do my best.

Mom is funniest when she makes faces.

**Suggested Endings:**
The most terrific thing about Mom . . .
No matter what, Mom always . . .

---

• As a Mother's Day gift, have your students make this book with a cover that is shaped and decorated like their mom's face.

• Present these books to Mom at a class Mother's Day tea.

• Incorporate science by studying moms throughout the animal kingdom.

---

# Save The Earth
## (Whole-Group Book)

### Make children aware of our fragile environment.

**Format:** Teach students environmental awareness. Then write letters of concern in the form of a book and send them to an elected official. (We wrote ours to the President!)

**Examples:**

> Dear Mr. President,
> Would you please tell the company that makes plastic bags to stop! Because boaters take their lunch in them and throw them in the water. Sea animals eat them and die.
> Your friend,
> Sheyna

> Dear Mr. President,
> This letter is about the environment. The ozone layer has holes in it already from aerosol cans. Please help stop making aerosol cans.
> Your friend,
> Tim

> Save The Earth!

---

• Since letter-writing skills may be too advanced for younger children, you could simply have your students write one concern about the environment on each page.

• Visit a recycling center for a class field trip.

• Have your students design environmental awareness posters to place around your school.

# Animals Around Us
## (Individual Book)

### What animals are native to your area?

**Format:** Study the animals that live in your region. Write about them in this book.

**Examples:**

Flamingos have a long neck, and they are pink.

Alligators are very strong, and they have sharp teeth.

**Suggested Endings:**

My favorite animal is . . .

The most interesting animal is _____ because . . .

• Students could research one specific animal and write their book in report form.

• This is great time for incorporating the use of nonfiction books in the classroom. A wonderful teacher reference book on this subject is Beverly Kobrin's *Eyeopeners!*

# Adventures In
_____ Grade

**(Individual Book)**

## Look back at a great school year.

**Format:** Students write about their favorite memories of the past school year.

**Examples:**

**Suggested Endings:**
The best thing about _____ grade . . .
I hope next year . . .

- This book would make a great "big book" to leave for next year's class.

- You may wish to add "yearbook" pages to this book such as autograph pages, student photos, class prophecies, and interviews with special people in the school.

- You could share these books at an end-of-the-year picnic.

# Independent Writing Activities

Our writing ideas, up to this point, have been mainly teacher-directed. It is important, however, to set aside some time each day for independent writing as well. This allows your students to apply the skills they are learning through teacher-directed activities. It also gives you an opportunity to evaluate and assess more accurately, and on an individual basis.

This section explains two simple ways to implement independent writing in your classrooms: Journals and Creative Writing Books. We use the activities alternately throughout the week. For example, one of the activities is used on Monday, Wednesday, and Friday. The other activity is used on Tuesday and Thursday.

## Journals

Wait! Don't close the book! We, too, have experienced the disease "Journal Phobia." But we think we've found the cure.

Many teachers have started journals and given them up, or never started them at all, because of the extra work that is involved.

For example:

a. putting journals together

b. getting students motivated to write in them

c. writing back to every student each day.

But there are many positive outcomes when students write in journals. They have an opportunity to apply their writing skills in a nonevaluative and therefore nonthreatening situation. They also get an opportunity to share private thoughts with the teacher that otherwise they would never share. This, in turn, gives the teacher a unique chance to get to know each child in a special way.

If we promise to give you easy solutions to overcome the negative aspects of journals, will you promise to give them another try?

# Here goes . . .

1. Don't be burdened by putting together elaborate, expensive journals. Make them as simple as you can. Here are some examples:

a. spiral-bound note pads
b. notebook paper stapled inside construction paper
c. half-sized bound booklets (spiral bound, with oak tag covers and mimeographed pages (see page 54)

2. Don't intimidate your students with full-sized paper! They will think they are expected to fill the whole page. This turns them off. Can you blame them? Use half-sized pages and you will be amazed at the difference.

3. Don't get writer's cramp trying to write back to your students each day. By having them write every other day, you obviously won't be responding as often. We answer each child only once a week.

However, we do encourage writing back to students, at least at first, so that they can get a sense of what journals are. But at some point you may wish to allow your students' journals to become private. (Your students may want this also!) At this time, you may stop answering them altogether, and just read the journals. Your students may even want you to stop reading their journals. One suggestion is to have two journal boxes, one marked "PLEASE READ" and one marked "PLEASE DO NOT READ"!

Journal writing can be fun. Give our ideas a try. You will be glad you did!

## Creative Writing Booklets

This is a writing activity that is independent, brief, and highly appealing. Our students love it and so do we!

On the days that we don't use journals, our students write endings to sentence starters. (Note: The students are not expected to write a story, just complete a sentence creatively.) Each child has a booklet made with 5"x 8" index cards, spiral-bound with a cover (or simply tied together with yarn). The sentence starter is written on the chalkboard. Each student copies the sentence starter onto the index card and finishes it with a creative ending.

## Here are 30 ideas to get you started:

1. If I had one more week of summer vacation . . .
2. The best thing about school is . . .
3. One thing I like to do at home is . . .
4. I'm afraid of . . .
5. My favorite animals are . . .
6. If I could fly . . .
7. The scariest thing I ever saw was . . .
8. My parents . . .
9. A good friend is someone who . . .
10. If I had a secret cave . . .
11. If I was in a bad storm . . .
12. My favorite things to eat are . . .
13. One adventure I would like to go on . . .
14. I'm thankful for . . .
15. Autumn is when . . .
16. You should see my . . .
17. Christmas is a time for . . .
18. Winter is great because . . .
19. My family likes to . . .
20. If my friend was an alien . . .
21. My favorite dog . . .
22. My magic unicorn . . .
23. Last night I dreamed . . .
24. Someone told me . . .
25. The prettiest flower I ever saw . . .
26. Springtime makes me want to . . .
27. Rainy days . . .
28. When I play in the sun . . .
29. If I rode in the Space Shuttle . . .
30. On summer vacation . . .

# RESOURCES

## WRITING

Atwell, Nancie. *In the Middle: Writing, Reading, and Learning with Adolescents*. Portsmouth, NH: Heinemann, 1987.

_____, ed. *Workshop 1 by and for Teachers: Writing and Literature*. Portsmouth, NH: Heinemann, 1989.

_____. *Coming to Know: Writing to Learn in the Middle Grades*. Portsmouth, NH: Heinemann, 1990.

Baghban, Marcia. *Our Daughter Learns to Read and Write*. Newark, DE: International Reading Association, 1985.

Barron, Marlene. *I Learn to Read and Write the Way I Learn to Talk*. Katonah, NY: Richard C. Owen Publishers, 1990.

Baskwill, Jane, and Whitman, Paulette. *A Guide to Classroom Publishing*. Toronto, Ont.: Scholastic TAB, 1988.

Bean, Wendy, and Bouffler, Christine. *Spell by Writing*. Portsmouth, NH: Heinemann, 1988.

Bissex, Glenda. *GNYS AT WRK*. Cambridge, MA: Harvard University Press, 1980.

Buchanan, Ethel. *Spelling for the Whole Language Classroom*. Winnipeg, Man.: The C.E.L. Group, 1989.

Butler, Andrea, and Turbill, Jan. *Towards a Reading-Writing Classroom*. Portsmouth, NH: Heinemann, 1984.

Calkins, Lucy McCormick. *Lessons from a Child: On the Teaching and Learning of Writing*. Portsmouth, NH: Heinemann, 1983.

_____. *The Art of Teaching Writing*. Portsmouth, NH: Heinemann, 1986.

_____. *Living Between the Lines*. Portsmouth, NH: Heinemann, 1991.

Cambourne, Brian and Turbill, Jan. *Coping with Chaos*. Portsmouth, NH: Heinemann, 1987.

Clay, Marie. *What Did I Write?* Portsmouth, NH: Heinemann, 1975.

_____. *Writing Begins at Home*. Portsmouth, NH: Heinemann, 1988.

Cochrane, Orin, et al. *Reading, Writing, and Caring*. Katonah, NY: Richard C. Owen Publishers, 1985.

Collerson, John, ed. *Writing for Life*. Portsmouth, NH: Heinemann, 1988.

Dakos, Kalli. *What's There to Write About?* New York: Scholastic, 1989.

Frank, Marjorie. *If You're Trying to Teach Kids How to Write, You Gotta Have This Book!* Nashville, TN: Incentive Publications, 1979.

Fulwiler, Toby, ed. *The Journal Book.* Portsmouth, NH: Heinemann, 1987.

Gentry, J. Richard. *Spel . . . Is a Four-Letter Word.* Portsmouth, NH: Heinemann, 1987.

Gordon, Naomi, ed. *Classroom Experiences: The Writing Process in Action.* Portsmouth, NH: Heinemann, 1984.

Graves, Donald. *Writing: Teachers and Children at Work.* Portsmouth, NH: Heinemann, 1983.

_____. *A Researcher Learns to Write.* Portsmouth, NH: Heinemann, 1984.

_____. *Experiment with Fiction.* Portsmouth, NH: Heinemann, 1989.

_____. *Investigate Nonfiction.* Portsmouth, NH: Heinemann, 1989.

_____. *Discover Your Own Literacy.* Portsmouth, NH: Heinemann, 1990.

_____. *Build a Literate Classroom.* Portsmouth, NH: Heinemann, 1991.

Graves, Donald and Stuart, Virginia. *Write from the Start.* New York: New American Library, 1985.

Hall, Nigel, and Robinson, Anne. *"Some Day You Will No All About Me": Young Children's Explorations in the World of Letters.* Portsmouth, NH: Heinemann, 1991.

Hansen, Jane. *When Writers Read.* Portsmouth, NH: Heinemann, 1987.

Hansen, Jane; Newkirk, Thomas; and Graves, Donald. *Breaking Ground: Teachers Relate Reading and Writing in the Elementary School.* Portsmouth, NH: Heinemann, 1985.

Harste, Jerome, and Short, Kathy. *Creating Classrooms for Authors: The Reading-Writing Connection.* Portsmouth, NH: Heinemann, 1988.

Harste, Jerome; Woodward, Virginia; and Burke, Carolyn. *Language Stories & Literacy Lessons.* Portsmouth, NH: Heinemann, 1984.

Heard, Georgia. *For the Good of the Earth and Sun: Teaching Poetry.* Portsmouth, NH: Heinemann, 1989.

Hill, Mary. *Home: Where Reading and Writing Begin.* Portsmouth, NH: Heinemann, 1989.

Holly, Mary Louise. *Writing to Know: Keeping a Personal-Professional Journal.* Portsmouth, NH: Heinemann, 1989.

Hubbard, Ruth. *Authors of Pictures, Draughtsmen of Words.* Portsmouth, NH: Heinemann, 1989.

Kitagawa, Mary, and Kitagawa, Chisato. *Making Connections with Writing: An Expressive Writing Model in Japanese Schools.* Portsmouth, NH: Heinemann, 1987.

Lamme, Linda. *Growing Up Writing*. Reston, VA: Acropolis Books, 1984.

Lloyd, Pamela. *How Writers Write*. Portsmouth, NH: Heinemann, 1987.

McCracken, Robert and Marlene. *Stories, Songs and Poetry to Teach Reading and Writing*. Chicago: American Library Association, 1986.

_____. *Reading, Writing and Language: A Practical Guide for Primary Teachers*. Winnipeg, Man.: Peguis, 1979.

McVitty, Walter. *Getting It Together: Organizing the Reading-Writing Classroom*. Portsmouth, NH: Heinemann, 1986.

Myers, Miles. *The Teacher-Researcher: How to Study Writing in the Classroom*. Urbana, IL: National Council of Teachers of English, 1985.

Newman, Judith. *The Craft of Children's Writing*. Portsmouth, NH: Heinemann, 1985.

Newkirk, Thomas. *More Than Stories: The Range of Children's Writing*. Portsmouth, NH: Heinemann, 1989.

Parry, Jo-Ann, and Hornsby, David. *Write On: A Conference Approach to Writing*. Portsmouth, NH: Heinemann, 1988.

Parsons, Les. *Response Journals*. Portsmouth, NH: Heinemann, 1989.

_____. *Writing in the Real Classroom*. Portsmouth, NH: Heinemann, 1991.

Perl, Sondra. *Through Teachers' Eyes: Portraits of Writing Teachers at Work*. Portsmouth, NH: Heinemann, 1986.

Rhodes, Lynn, and Dudley-Marling, Curt. *Readers and Writers with a Difference: A Holistic Approach to Teaching Learning Disabled and Remedial Students*. Portsmouth, NH: Heinemann, 1988.

Routman, Regie. *Transitions: From Literature to Literacy*. Portsmouth, NH: Heinemann, 1988.

_____. *Invitations*. Portsmouth, NH: Heinemann, 1991.

Schickendanz, Judith. *Adam's Righting Revolutions*. Portsmouth, NH: Heinemann, 1990.

Smith, Frank. *Writing and the Writer*. New York: Holt, Rinehart & Winston, 1982.

Temple, Charles, et al. *The Beginnings of Writing*. Boston: Allyn & Bacon, 1988.

Turbill, Jan, ed. *No Better Way to Teach Writing!* Portsmouth, NH: Heinemann, 1982.

_____. *Now, We Want to Write!* Portsmouth, NH: Heinemann, 1983.

## WHOLE LANGUAGE

Buros, Jay. *Why Whole Language?* Rosemont, NJ: Programs for Education, 1991.

Edelsky, Carole; Altwerger, Bess; and Flores, Barbara. *Whole Language: What's the Difference?* Portsmouth, NH: Heinemann, 1991.

Eisele, Beverly. *Managing the Whole Language Classroom.* Cypress, CA: Creative Teaching Press, 1991.

Goodman, Kenneth. *What's Whole in Whole Language.* Portsmouth, NH: Heinemann, 1986.

Goodman, Kenneth; Goodman, Yetta; and Hood, Wendy. *whole Language Evaluation Book.* Portsmouth, NH: Heinemann, 1988.

Holdaway, Don. *Foundations of Literacy.* New York: Scholastic, 1979.

Merrilees, Cindy and Haack, Pamela. *Ten Ways To Become A Better Reader.* Cleveland, OH: Modern Curriculum Press, 1991.

Mills, Heidi, and Clyde, Jean Anne. *Portraits of a Whole Language Classroom.* Portsmouth, NH: Heinemann, 1990.

Newman, Judith. *Whole Language: Theory in Use.* Portsmouth, NH: Heinemann, 1985.

*SDE Sourcebook III – Transitions.* Peterborough, NH: The Society for Developmental Education, 1990.

*SDE Sourcebook IV – The Child's Window to the World.* Peterborough, NH: The Society for Developmental Education, 1991.

*SDE Sourcebook V – Into Teachers' Hands.* Peterborough, NH: The Society for Developmental Education, 1992.

## About The Authors

In addition to teaching elementary school, Cindy Merrilees and Pamela Haack stay busy conducting local seminars, writing books, and working as national education consultants for The Society for Developmental Education. Their practical ideas for teaching reading and writing can also be found in their first book, *Ten Ways To Become A Better Reader.*